BREAKING
Cycles of
DYSFUNCTION

BREAKING Cycles of DySFUNCTION

REGINALD & SHANIKA WINGFIELD ED.S.

Breaking Cycles of Dysfunction

ISBN: 9798682500109

TABLE  CONTENTS

Introduction 1

Family 4

Work 27

Relationships/Marriages 34

Personality Traits 46

How to Break Cycles 57

How to Manage Dysfunctional People (Functional Balance) 71

How NOT to "Manage" Dysfunction 76

Hashtags 79

The Plan 83

Notes 85

About the Authors 88

CHAPTER 1

INTRODUCTION

Have you ever wondered why you engage in certain behaviors? Have you looked back at your family and saw similar dysfunctional ways? Do you process the thought or automatically assume that it's normal? After more than 20 years of experience in this field, we have learned that most people are unaware that they operate in cycles of dysfunction. As a solution, and a way to help people recognize these behaviors, we will discuss ways to help identify dysfunctional cycles. This thought-provoking book will have you question things in your life to identify the areas of dysfunction that need to be broken.

Breaking cycles of dysfunction became a mandate for us when we saw how necessary it was to break away from the dysfunctional aspects of our upbringing. Not all things dysfunctional were obvious at first, but along the way, we were made aware of certain things and found it vital to break through them one step at a time.

We are committed to sharing aspects of our own lives, so that you can find ways to acknowledge and tackle your own cycles of dysfunction. This book will ensure that you are clear with what dysfunctions run through your blood line, with Biblical and practical ways of breaking them to ensure you operate in purpose and that your destiny is not hindered in any way. It will also allow future generations to not be stricken with these same dysfunctions and safeguard their future.

Dysfunction is the killer of God's plans for your life. This may or may not be a salvation issue, but it will impede on the quality of life you live. It will also deter the quality of life your children will have. Throughout this book dysfunction will be defined as an abnormality or impairment in the function of a specified system, and or deviation from the norms of social behavior in a way regarded as bad or detrimental. When we take these two descriptions of the term, you will be able to see how certain cycles and patterns in your life have been or are dysfunctional in nature; and in what manner it has adversely affected your life.

Also remember dysfunction is not just behaviors. It can manifest as thoughts, attitudes, ways of doing things. It can show up in your physical health, mental health, how you cope with stress as well as how you handle things in everyday life. When looking at dysfunction holistically, it can and will show up in many facets of your life. Our suggestion is when starting this journey in recognizing and breaking these cycles is to tackle one issue at a time. At best, if you see a dysfunction that is operating in more than one area, it is acceptable to confront that specific thing and then adjust in the areas it has affected. For example, if you (or family) deal with not respecting authority. You can find yourself being fired from multiple jobs or have a challenge keeping a job. This will affect the financial stability in your home, and subsequent the quality of your life. Once you uproot the issue of why you do not respect authority, break completely away from it, then you can process through the financial issues and your quality of life. To further explain, you will have a consistent and stable job that provides. Your home life will in turn become stable financially. Bills will be paid on time. You won't stress about things being turned off or face evictions, etc. Now you can live without the fear of what will happen when the money stops coming. This case may seem extreme; however, we have seen tons of people who deal with one dysfunctional aspect that plagues multiple areas of their lives.

CHAPTER 2

FAMILY

Have you ever seen families troubled by the same things? As we look back on families, we are familiar with, there is always a family resemblance. That likeness can be either good or bad, positive or negative, nonetheless, it is very present. Even the most positive things can be dysfunctional in nature if you discern the root of a behavior. For instance, if you see a family that are workaholics. This can be seen as very positive. A family who enjoys working. However, what is the family unit like? Are they working so much that they are neglectful in other areas. It is fine to work and enjoy working, but there needs to be functional balance. In this chapter, which may be the longest chapter in this book, we will discuss how the family unit can be dysfunctional and ways to break those cycles.

Look at your family unit in great depth, and with a sober mind. This will be the only way to see what areas objectively and clearly are consistent in your life and family. It may be difficult, triggering, or you may feel downright angry about it once it comes to the light. It is not complicated in some instances to look at your family and see what the issues are, the only challenge is for people to acknowledge out loud what they are, and then to do something about it. Who wants to pick apart their family issues or be the person to say what is really plaguing the family? It may be a daunting task, but it is necessary to acknowledge in order to break them. And yes, there may come resistance, misunderstandings, denials, rejections, and abandonments in some cases, but it is necessary to start the journey of breaking the cycles.

Asking yourself questions out loud will help you recognize the dysfunctions that trouble your family. If you are having difficulties pointing out what those cycles may be, ask yourself these questions: What ways do your family cope or handle situations that are dysfunctional? Do you get angry? Do you physically fight? Or do you want to cuss and get revenge? Do you just sweep things under the rug and act like nothing ever happened?

This is just one set of questions that will prompt you to think about what areas of dysfunction flows through your family. Below there will be examples of three families. These families are from real life situations, and actual names are withheld for privacy. We will be using the seven steps to help break cycles of dysfunction. You will find the steps in more detail, and how to use them in chapter six.

Family 1: Divorced/Unmarried

How many people know families where most or all of the members are divorced or unmarried? And not just divorced once, but multiple times. This case will come with two different examples. One that has been divorced several times, and the other with multiple unmarried (with children) members.

The Holland and Spencer families have been inundated by the same issue…divorce! Divorce is not a horrible thing in and of itself but when it becomes habitual and without (obvious) reason, it is dysfunctional.

Sarah Holland is the most loving, and caring person we have the privilege of knowing. She comes from a strong supportive family that is rooted in the church and community. The family is women heavy meaning, there are more women than men for whatever reason. What is noticeable is although the women are strong, loving, caring, attentive, they have been divorced several times. In some cases, these women have children by one man and then divorce shortly after that which leaves them to be a single parent. After years of being single, they find themselves in another marriage that ends shortly in divorce. The CDC (Center for Disease Control) marriage statistics in America reports the divorce rate is about 45%. Subsequent marriages and divorces percentages increase to 67% for the second, and 75% will end in divorce with the third.[1] Sarah grew up watching her grandmother, mother, aunts and cousins go through the same defeat. It was heartbreaking to see Sarah fall into the same trap. In her mid-20s with a husband and children, on the brink of divorce. It happened, and as was stated before, for reasons unknown. Both people were good people. They were educated, loving, kind, attentive, but could not see the dysfunction that ran rampant in her family. Did she just fall into the cycle? It appears to be so.

Sarah found herself in marriage number two. The same ingredients were apparent, loving, kind, and motivated individuals. Not even a year went by, and divorce is already imminent. The signs were there, but was it obvious to Sarah? If she saw the dysfunctional marriages in her family, would she have been able to stop it? We believe it is possible to see a train wreck about to happen and get off the track to safety.

After divorce number two was concrete, Sarah finds herself single for a while with growing children. She is progressing in every area of her life but when it comes to intimate relationships, it has been pressing. There is an unforeseen challenge that comes into every romantic relationship she finds herself in.

Holly Spencer has found herself in the same situation as Sarah but there is a slight difference. Although Holly's family are church-going, religious people, multiple divorces have been the center of most women in her family as well. Holly watched her grandparents in a loving marriage for many decades. These two were the patriarch and matriarch of the family unit. They gave birth to several children, mostly girls, and raised them in the church. Again, for reasons unknown, and without looking deeper, the women grew up with hateful attitudes and angry dispositions. They were very talented at music, but people did not want to be around them for very long. This transferred into their marriages. It cannot be speculated or assumed that their husbands were without fault, but to demonstrate the point, it is obvious what the women contributed to the relationship and their responsibility in the marriage. It was also witnessed that these women found themselves in adulterous relationships while married, and with other married men.

To give more details with the Spencer family, the men (Uncles to Holly) were also in extramarital relationships, but it did not affect their marriages like their female siblings. In order to see this cycle of dysfunction you have to eliminate the stable marriage they knew growing up. For reasons unknown, it crept into their generation and bled into the subsequent. That is where Holly picks up. Although she did not participate in any illicit relationships, she became angry and unpleasant to be around. It left her three times divorced with six children and alone before she turned 30 years old. If she had noticed the patterns of dysfunction with her family, would it have saved her marriages? We believe so.

We are fully aware that people subscribe to their own belief systems and function from those standards whether we agree or not. With that being said, the next family without any religious or moral standards presented, is an example of how every woman in the family is unmarried but with multiple children, and in some cases, multiple fathers.

The Miller family was a well-connected, close, and loving family. The patriarch and matriarch integrated a closeness with their 20 children that was needed immediately after the early death of them both. The children stuck together at their young age, but it fell apart for reasons unidentified when they became adults. They all grew up knowing how stable the marriage of their parents was but failed to have that same thing in their lives. Out of 20 children, there were 15 girls and 5 boys, and only one of the children is married. Generations later, Christian Miller is happily married with children.

He looks back at the generations before him and realizes his aunts, uncles and cousins don't see each other and none of them are married. However, they all have children. He has seen generations of family members live unmarried but with the desire to do so. How could he break the cycle of that dysfunction but not the rest of them? It was because Christian decided to acknowledge the magnitude of that cycle and work at breaking it.

Christian's story is a perfect example of taking these steps to break cycles of dysfunction. The steps include Acknowledge/Expose, Confront, Renounce, Deliverance (Stop what you're doing), Replace with Holy Spirit, Find/Create new behaviors, attitudes, (Biblically/Scripturally sound) and have great Accountability. If you do not subscribe to Christian principles, there is still practical ways to help break cycles of dysfunction. But first, we will apply the set of steps to these three family examples.

- Acknowledging and exposing multiple divorces and unmarried couples with children is the beginning of the process. This step does not have to be a public announcement, or even a declaration made to your family. It is simply just the action of saying to yourself out loud what you are exposing. For example, "Every woman in my family have been divorced multiple times." After that simple confession, it is time to confront it.

- Confronting a situation that seems invisible can be challenging, however, it is important to not neglect this step. As you will learn more in Chapter six, confronting is a step where you face what has occurred. If there are close family members who are open for dialogue, you can discuss with them their perspective on why the cycles have been established and progressed. If not, seeking out wise counsel elsewhere will be beneficial.

- Renounce and deliverance may seem like religious terms, but it simply means to, "formally declare one's abandonment of something and the action of being rescued or set free." Everyone is free to endorse these words and their descriptions. You will have to abandon and be set free from the manifestations of multiple divorces and the urge to be coupled up and unmarried.

- For those who are believers of Jesus Christ, it is vital that when you have been set free from an undesired behavior to fill those areas with Holy Spirit. Then those specific areas will be dedicated to Him, giving Him full reign over them.

- Find and create new behaviors and attitudes that are Biblically/Scripturally sound will be necessary. It will help build a foundation that will help you be successful. For instance, saying and implementing not getting connected with people romantically until there is an understanding of purpose for that relationship. And if it is not, leave it alone. Do not further the relational inquiry.

- Accountability is sometimes a hard pill to swallow…and keep down! In this situation it will be crucial to have someone close and wise to tell you to not to pursue a relationship when you are not healthy enough to sustain it or in a place to financially run a household. There can be numerous areas that need to be checked in order to not fall into the trap of multiple divorces or becoming coupled unmarried. The more leeway an accountability partner may have with you is better.

- The areas that are religiously focused, Renounce/Deliverance, Fill with Holy Spirit and Replace with Biblically/Scripturally sound areas can be changed into: Renounce/Remain free from, and fill with positive and acceptable behaviors. It is not a significant change but rather something anyone can adopt. Remaining free from using this example would be to not indulge in unproductive relationships.

Family 2: Manipulative/Controlling (Abandonment/Rejection)

Have you seen families where the older generations are very good (joking, but serious) at persuading others to do what they want them to do, without regard to what that person really wants to do? That was a loaded question but hopefully you get it. Being good at persuasion is not necessarily bad or dysfunctional, but this art can be rooted in manipulation and control. There are tons of theories on why that is. We won't focus too much on the roots but have counseled people who are manipulative and controlling deal with high levels of abandonment and rejection. Although there is understanding and, in some instances, compassion to why these things have occurred, it becomes tremendously dysfunctional when a person feels they have the right to manipulate and control someone else's destiny, plans, desires, decisions, and life. Meet the Cargill and James families.

Sheila Cargill grew up in a family that lived on what people thought of their family. The image of their family structure was far more important to them than dealing with what was actually going on inside. It was dysfunctional, putting it lightly, downright violent and mentally taxing. It did not matter to her parents what was being swept under the rug. All that mattered was that people believed the lying image they put out. If that was intact, nothing else was a concern. They wanted to control the narrative. Not sure if it was because they did not want accountability, criminal probing, social services inquiries or if it would put a dent in the image, they worked hard at showing. Whatever the case, they thrived on manipulating and controlling Sheila and her siblings, especially the image they worked so hard at securing. It did not seem like control at first, but 'ways of doing things'. When things were strongly suggested, not adhered too, there was hell to pay. Hell came in the way of psychological and financial abuse and forceful, violent conversations. When those things did not work, they went on a smear campaign against Sheila. They fed friends and family members with lies that made them turn their backs on her. Sheila realized a little later in life the cycle of dysfunction that was at play. She noticed that if she did not comply with their wants or needs, there would be instant consequences. And for the siblings who did comply with the manipulation, they were rewarded.

It became clear that the cycle of dysfunction her parents operate in has flowed through her siblings, and their families. Instead of looking outside of themselves, discerning what is going on, and even investigating to know the truth, they sit in the counsel of the manipulative and follow their negative and dysfunctional behavior towards her. It was obvious to those that benefit from the dysfunction, maybe unwilling to part from it. But for those like Sheila, who knows there are no benefits to dysfunction, will be diligent to break them and live a happy and fulfilled life. Although breaking out of the dysfunction brought more hatred towards Sheila, she was willing to be the breaker of dysfunctional cycles for her own family. We will discuss how she broke out and stayed out even when things continue to be dysfunctional towards her.

Parker James came from a very similar family. The only difference between the two families is that he was still somewhat connected with his family in proximity. It is slightly more difficult to see the cycles of dysfunction when you are still within the family dynamic. When you feel obligated to be in their company, it can become a struggle to see the truth for what it really is. And the obligation derived from the power the parents put on him through words and behaviors.

What kept occurring is Parker's parents believed what they wanted mattered more than what he wanted. And not just him, the other siblings as well, but the brunt of control was over Parker. They wanted to control what he did, while manipulating him to fulfil their wants, desires, and material needs. This is even more stressful when the person who recognizes the dysfunction has a loving heart. Sometimes that loving heart pulls towards the dysfunction to not expose what is really going on because they do not want to cause pain, division, or strife. Nevertheless, Parker came to terms with how dysfunctional his family is and was determined not to allow the cycle to bleed through his own family. He even saw it with his siblings. And since they were not willing to see the manipulative and controlling behaviors from their parents, they all ostracized him. Their relationship is strained but Parker understands why. Even though his siblings may not be in a place to see the truth, he has loved them without condition and has implemented boundaries to keep him and his family protected.

With both families, it was acknowledged that the parents dealt heavily with being abandoned by their parents in some form or fashion. They were given up at an early age. Given to other family members to be taken care of. And in some instances, they weren't given up physically but abandoned and rejected emotionally. They had to grow up quickly and establish things on their own without the loving support of family. They also came from very dysfunctional settings. And in their cases, did not see the dysfunction for what it was. That led to them not acknowledging it and stopping it with their families. It bled right into their immediate and subsequent families. It was as if they had blinders on to the pain they went through and were not determined to change things.

Maybe they didn't have the fortitude to do it? Maybe they weren't aware of their dysfunctional behaviors. What if they didn't want to come to terms with what their pain caused their children? There are a ton of questions and statements that can be asked in these scenarios. The hope is that there is help. There are strategies that can help someone see the dysfunction that has run rampant in their lives. It is as simple as being sober-minded and honest about what you have been through, what you have caused because of that, and what to do moving forward. Let's look at these two families and see how the steps to break cycles of dysfunction can be applied.

- Acknowledging and exposing the cycles of dysfunction in these examples will start with accepting what they endured as children. As stated above, and without explaining too much, the roots stem from what they experienced in their rearing. Again, this step does not have to be a public announcement, or even a declaration made to your family, however it can be therapeutic in the right settings. In a professional counseling session, it can be safe to speak on what you're acknowledging in order to move to the next step. If you are unable to be in a professional counseling space, it is vital to recognize what the dysfunction is to move forward.

- Confronting this type of situation can be extremely challenging. Most people who are comfortable in their dysfunctional behaviors will do anything to keep it functioning. Although very difficult, it is important to not neglect this step. Like in example number one, if there are close family members who are open for dialogue, you can discuss with them their perspective on why the cycles have been established and progressed. If not, seeking out wise counsel will be beneficial.

- Renounce what you have suffered. Leave it behind in thought and deed. Stay far from behaviors and attitudes that are very familiar. Even when it becomes very difficult. It will be tough to set boundaries and enforce them, however it is vital in this stage. Holidays, family gatherings, and other events will look different, so it is important to have a plan for these interactions. For example, you may want to refrain from going to their house but a ten-minute facetime to say hello to family may work. If it is too challenging to facetime or speak, know that you are not obligated to be surrounded by anyone who is toxic, dysfunctional, or abusive.

- Filling those seemingly empty spaces with the Holy Spirit will be imperative in this time. There will be times of questioning your decisions to break free from family cycles of dysfunction. What is more important is to know that you stay in the truth that God offers. Keep his scriptures close to your heart so in times of desperation to go back, or hopelessness, you can cling to what is lovely, pure and of good report.

- Finding new and creative ways to enjoy your family without dysfunction can be challenging at first. However, the sky is the limit on how you can establish new traditions and introduce new ways of doing things. Remember, this step is extremely valuable for your family and subsequent generations. What you create at this juncture will be what is carried on. Make it Godly! And make it good.

- Accountability will be a staple in this time. What to look for when seeking accountability is partners or a village who are mentally, physically, and spiritually stable. There are no way people who are not stable can help you become and stay stable. When you are having a lapse in judgment or having a weak moment, they can and will assist. It is also important that your partners or village have permission to keep you accountable. A thorough conversation about what it looks like will be pertinent in the beginning, and follow-up conversations when things have moved forward. Accountability looks different at different stages.

Family 3: Constant Fighting/Inability to Resolve Conflict

"I've been fighting my whole life. I don't know what else to do but to fight. I fight with my hands and with my mouth!" It is certain that you know someone who has uttered these very words. We all know people who fight. We are even familiar with people who were considered good fighters in their neighborhoods growing up. Fighting and the inability to resolve conflict properly can stem from generations of insecurities and traumas. But as stated previously, there are reasons some people feel the need to fight physically and verbally, but we will not get into those in this book.

At any stage in life, there will be a need to fight and handle conflict. Not physically or verbally fighting but a fight (a push, challenge, struggle) to get through certain stages in life or situations. We are all born with an innate fight or flight button. When put in situations, our bodies tell us to fight through this thing, or run from it. The dysfunction happens when there is not a healthy process to resolve conflict. Some people believe that resolving conflict is to fight about it. There is no mature, methodical, mental plan that stirs up when faced with conflict. Instead, anger is released through something they are in control of, their hands, mouth or both.

This dysfunctional cycle bleeds through generations and is usually not recognized until that 5-year-old kindergartener is fighting in his classroom with no obvious reasons why. It will stop the fighter in their tracks almost immediately in some cases. They may even violently ask why the 5-year-old is fighting while simultaneously neglecting the fact that they taught them to do it. It can be eye-opening to see yourself, your dysfunctional behaviors replay in the lives of your small children. The mature thing to do is recognize the cycle, acknowledge the why, and start the healing process. And not just for the initial fighter, but for their children too.

There is no family example of this scenario because we all know people and families like this. Learning to resolve conflict is a skill. It needs to be taught in a healthy and safe place. When that is void, it leads to making negative decisions that causes even more conflict. USA reports in October 2022 that there were 284.4 aggravated assaults per 100,000 people in 2021.[2] As soon as one identifies the causes to their inability to resolve conflict, they can work on breaking it. Below are examples in each step on how to do that.

- Acknowledging and exposing the cycles of dysfunction will look like sitting in a quiet place reflecting on all of the fights (physical and verbal) you have had or can remember. Begin to write down the details of those fights. For example, being cut off in traffic, or passed over for a job promotion. Acknowledge how those things made you feel. Then write down why it made you feel that way. Next you will expose the detail in each situation because more than likely, there will be similarities or a common denominator. Confessing your faults in these situations will push you to the next step.

- Confronting this type of situation can be severely emotional. So, if you are not emotionally intelligent enough to handle exposing it, it would be safe to have someone present to aid in this process. It may be more beneficial to confront the dysfunction in a safe place with people you love rather than with the people you learned the dysfunction from. It may cause more conflict for you because they may not be in a place to receive such revelation. They also may not be in a place to confront their own dysfunctions and may be unwilling to change. If you find yourself in this situation, it is best to keep this step private. And what we mean by private is, make it a point to know personally (with other safe people) that you have confronted the issues and patterns that are dysfunctional and are on a path to change it.

- Renouncing the reasons why you fight will be a cleansing process. It will relieve you from the responsibility of dealing with dysfunction involuntarily. A lot of times we blame ourselves for things we picked up in childhood. However, we must renounce our part in the continuance of it. That role we played is our responsibility to tackle. It is also our duty to leave it behind. Learn from it, and at the appropriate time share with others how you've overcome it.

- Finding new and creative ways to handle conflict and stop fighting can look like signing up for a class that teaches health conflict resolutions or a boxing gym. Many people have taken their physical fighting skills to the ring. For example, Mike Tyson. It is well known that he publicly shares how he was bullied and fought a lot growing up. Instead of hiding or becoming the bully, he rendered his skill to the experienced fighters and became a professional boxer. Not every former fighter will become the next heavy weight champion of the world, however, you can find a new skill set that will help you to alleviate those painful memories of fighting, the desire to continue to fight, as well as assist in learning healthy conflict resolutions.

- Accountability must be strong in this area. It may feel like you have to rid yourself of those around you that like to fight and can't handle conflict, but it will benefit you in the long run. Being accountable to someone who does not operate in the dysfunction you are now free from will help you to see things differently. There may be an accountability partner that was free from this cycle of dysfunction but has been grounded in the recovery and is available to help you along the journey. This will not only give you accountability but there will also be moments where you can learn from your partner.

Family Reflection Section:

I was watching a documentary about Bernie Madoff. It is a four-episode documentary on Netflix.[3] It was interesting to watch. For many years the Madoff Ponzi Scheme has been a topic of discussion. However, this documentary gives insight on how Bernie's desire for money, power, and prestige, which was dysfunctional, was the catalyst that destroyed thousands of people, families, and organizations. The need to people please and have power became so increasingly toxic that instead of taking a different approach to situations out of his control, he took a dysfunctional route. A route that did not cycle through his children but killed them. If you don't want the spoiler alert, stop reading now and go watch it! If you would like to see in real time how vital it is to break cycles of dysfunction, so you won't see in real time devastation, keep reading.

Bernie, the son of Jewish immigrants, grew up in the depression/war era where his parents struggled to keep food on the table, pay bills and keep jobs. His father went from job to job, while his mother stayed home. He incubated in struggle. Need was always around him. The longing to have more, do more, and be more was always present. It wasn't until his father moved them into the suburbs that he gained confidence in being the helper for other people. The answer and assistance someone else needed. It showed in his job as a lifeguard. It was also evident he wanted money by having side jobs. He was determined to do well, and not have the same struggles he watched his family go through.

While in school, he met his wife Ruth at the age of 13. Ruth came from money, power, and prestige. And to be adored by her family, he knew there was a level of power and stability he had to obtain to be accepted. This was the second turn of the wheel towards dysfunction.

With pressure and challenges from his father, and Ruth's family, Bernie spent one year in law school to please his father but then left. Struggle and failure roared with his parents while increasingly elevating the need for him not to fail as an adult. By any means necessary Bernie made this happen.

He wanted to be more successful than his father, and father-in-law. He set his eyes on how he could get an abundance of money and fast. Integrity and honesty were not part of the equation. At the pushing of his father-in-law, Bernie became a manager of people's monies. He stole their trust and their investments. He lived off what they gave, and he lied to them about their profits that never came to fruition. This cycle continued for decades. He included, with limited information to most, his immediate family, a brother, friends, and a host of other employees.

When the scheme became public, he was more concerned about how his name would be, rather than the trauma it caused thousands of people and his family. The dysfunctional thoughts of wanting to people please, hold power and be financially stable stripped those around him of their stability. It cycled through people that weren't even his family. The results were more harmful to his own family. As stated in the introduction, if you do not break cycles of dysfunction in your own life, it will be to the detriment of your children, and subsequent generations.

It was evident in Bernie's family. After he was convicted of the Ponzi scheme and sentenced to 150 years in federal prison, things started falling apart. The cycles of dysfunction that ran Bernie manifested in his sons' lives. The oldest son stricken with guilt and shame committed suicide on the 2-year anniversary of Bernie's arrest. The second son's cancer that he had beat 10-years prior came out of remission to kill him slowly. Ruth was more consumed by Bernie's dysfunction than anyone. Being connected to it since she was 13 years old caused her not to support her sons in their trying times, but to lean towards Bernie. It cost her everything. The Government ceased all her belongings except two suitcases full of clothes. She was removed from a seven-million-dollar penthouse to live in a 4-door Honda Civic.

The questions to ask are: If he was able to see the cycles of dysfunction he created for his own life, and stopped it before it was tangible, would it have saved thousands of victims, and his family? If there was sound wisdom and accountability at his disposal, would it have stopped earlier? The answer to these two questions is yes!

Yes, the breakdown of the cycles of dysfunction would have resulted in a different plan for his family and those he serviced. Although the cycles of dysfunction stopped (because of death) with his sons, it continues with his wife. And the trauma it caused the victims started a dysfunctional cycle for theirs.

There is a quote in the documentary that resonates deeply. It says, "The only people that can deceive you completely, are the people you trust completely. And the price of trusting anyone, is that they can betray you like that." -Diana B. Henriques

When we look at cycles of dysfunction and how they so richly and without hinderance flow through families for generations, it is safe to say, it's because family members trust so willingly. They are (and we all have been there) being deceived by generations of thoughts, behaviors, attitudes, traditions, ways of thinking and believing and it becomes their norm. It develops into a deviated system from what is tried and true. From what is sane, functional, and normal, to what is now dysfunctionally normal. Even though it may not have been intentionally malicious, it has become. Now it is time to break it!

Children in relation to their parents' section

As advocates for children and families, we would be remiss if there was not a section of this chapter specifically targeting children. Later in the book you will read how childhood dysfunctional behaviors continue with subsequent generations, however, it is crucial that we show the correlation between parent's dysfunctional cycles to that of their children. In most instances, people are unaware (or do not care), how their dysfunction affects other people to include their own children. Most parents we have encountered are oblivious to the behaviors their children mirror them with. Some parents are too late for the realization which leads children down a path of criminality versus someone upstanding. When we are faced with parents who have no clue where their children's criminal behavior comes from, we are forced to ask questions that lead to a quick discovery. Usually in the tune to, "who has a criminal background?" or "where you kicked out of school as a teenager?" When parents answer these questions, or anything similar, it is often helpful to get them to see how close the dysfunctional behaviors were, and how they had a hand in their children's dysfunctional cycles as well.

Many years ago, we dealt with a 13-year-old child in the Juvenile Justice System (JJS) who was court ordered to probation. We found out quickly that his father was also in the JJS as a teenager. Interestingly enough, they operated in the same dysfunctional behaviors. It is evident how dysfunctional thoughts, mindsets, and behaviors impact generations. Do you see the pattern? Based on our experience in this field, if parents aren't aware of their dysfunctional behaviors and are actively breaking them, they will fall onto their children. It will show up again if unacknowledged.

However, the other side is just as true. There will be times and instances that children develop dysfunctional cycles from their own traumas or mindsets. It's as if we're asking the old age question, "Which came first, the chicken or the egg?" We know that not every parent can be blamed or at fault for dysfunctional behaviors in their children. We also fully understand that it comes from somewhere. That point of reference may not be parents or families. It may be a friend. It may be a thought process they adopted on their own. Nevertheless, there will always be a starting point no matter where it came from. Digging up the root to where the dysfunction was born, especially if it is not familiar, should be first priority when dealing with children. When you read further, you will understand why it is important to stop these dysfunctional patterns in children quickly and early.

Segeren, Fassaert, de Wit and Popma researched and documented that,

> "Early onset of antisocial or criminal behavior, specifically before the age of 12, involvement in delinquency and drug use, negative or antisocial attitude and the accumulation of criminogenic factors, particularly over multiple domains, have been singled out as key determinants of persistence and escalation of criminal behavior into early adulthood."[4]

These are the cycles we are trying to break. It is crucial to the livelihood of young adults to have a successful foothold on life, especially in these early years. If not, they will waste more time trying to erase what has happened, or get from under what has happened, that it will rob them of young adult years. Children should be given the best chance at life, even if they made criminal and dysfunctional decisions. Helping them to be restored will be a vital addition in their lives. Kelly, Macy and Mears studied the recidivism rate of juveniles in Texas. They recognized how often juveniles come back into the system when there is a lack in risk and needs assessments.[5] The risks and needs assessments are just the beginning. There must be intentional engagement with the youth (and their family) in order for the assessments to be effective. Their study found that almost half of repeat offending juveniles, that had previous untreated mental health and substance abuse issues, did not receive treatment after their first offense.[5] This resulted in the juveniles reoffending. It confirms that when you don't deal with cycles of dysfunction holistically, there is cause for further problems.

*Some of the people who have been mentioned in this section have gone on to have successful marriages, relationships, and have set healthy boundaries with their extended family members, even if those family members still operate dysfunctionally.

CHAPTER 3

WORK

How do dysfunctional behaviors impact work relationships? Have you seen a co-worker become irate over something most would consider small? Work relationships may not be as intensive as family, and this chapter will not be as long as the previous one, but it will show you how cycles of dysfunction run rampant through your job and work relationships, or the lack thereof as well. It is important to note that these dysfunctional traits do not always begin in the workplace unless there was some initial trauma experienced there. It can be mentioned that if someone is operating in a dysfunctional way at work, it was established before their employment.

Have you heard the saying, "It's easier to fire a supervisor, than to find a whole new team of employees"? This saying refers to how a supervisor sets the tone of a workplace, and if employees are complaining about how horrible their supervisor is, it must have some truth to it. It also makes more sense to hire a supervisor, which is one person, than an entire team of employees. Nonetheless, we are not here to discuss workplace antics but how cycles of dysfunction can and will follow you to the workplace. Those same examples in the family section are not just family members. Most of them are working adults who go to the office every day with the same dysfunctions we have discussed.

In the United States, there is approximately 155 million people working.[6] Can you imagine how many of those people are functioning dysfunctional people? And how all of them need to break those cycles of dysfunction so they can have pleasant workplace environments. It is safe to assume that these hostile work environments derive from people who are dysfunctional in some form. The Dolman Law Group states,

> The term "hostile work environment" may seem self-explanatory. It's true that in a broad sense, a hostile work environment is an employment setting made uncomfortable by the behaviors, attitudes, and policies of employers and coworkers.[7]

With skill, compassion, and understanding it can be easy to discern why superiors or co-workers behave inappropriately. The skill of knowing why someone acts a certain way will come from years of experience. Having compassion and understanding does not give people a green light to continue in their dysfunctional behaviors, but it shows the misbehaved that people are genuinely concerned about them.

Most times when people in the workplace are behaving badly, it comes from dysfunctional patterns in their lives. In these situations, it is challenging to see how competent people cannot be in control of their behaviors. When we speak about competency, we are referencing the ability to gain knowledge through academics, trainings, and other necessary experiences but lack the awareness to see their own behaviors and how it affects their workplace and workplace relationships. In the example below, we will discuss Allison.

Allison is a certifiable professional. She went through years of schooling to be at the top of her field. Not only was she professional at the top of her career, along with working in corporate America, she operated her own business. Everything appeared to be going well within the first 3 weeks or so of a new assignment. After the honeymoon phase was over, we started to hear about the toxic work environment that was present. At first glance, someone meeting Allison for the first time would assume that she was there to uncover these toxic environments. Digging deeper into Allison's personality traits, as well as the dysfunctional cycles she inherited, one would consider maybe she is the dysfunction that entered the company. And that was confirmed when she was at job number five with the same story of how everyone else is dysfunctional, crazy and toxic. At that point, we knew an honest conversation needed to be had with her.

Allison gave us permission to be blatantly honest with our observations, and as a result, she came into awareness that it was her. She grew up in a household where her parents were dysfunctional and toxic in their marriage. There was also times Allison had an unhealthy emotional relationship with her mother. This gave Allison unconscious permission to connect and converse with superiors and authority figures as if she had authorization to do so. Allison believed it was okay to have relationships with superiors as if she was on the same level in the company. When the superiors would tell her she was out of line, there would be conflict. The conflict trickled down into the department was directing and it caused chaos throughout the company. Once Allison was in the highest position at another company, the unhealthy relationship connection would happen with the owners. The relationship did not begin unhealthy. Every employee needs a relationship with superiors, owners, and founders, however there must be clear boundaries. When those boundaries are crossed, it becomes apparent there is dysfunction operating. Remember Allison was taught by her mother to engage in an unhealthy relationship with a parent. This led Allison to have taken those learned behaviors into the workplace. When Allison crossed the boundaries with the owners of the new company, the dysfunction was in full operation. The same workplace dysfunction she used with other organizations was present. The owners started to see a different side of Allison and rendered her incompetent to run their company. Not because she wasn't more than qualified, but because she lacked discipline with her mouth (conversations, gossip, strife, etc.). She felt it was okay to speak with the owners in a tone that is reserved for same-level professional colleagues rather than those who have authority over you.

It took Allison a few lost jobs to realize she was the common denominator in all of those situations. It was tough for her to be faced with the truth; however, she learned the lesson quickly. She asked for help with steps on how to break the dysfunctional cycles, along with a strong and supportive accountability team. And within one year, she turned her dysfunctional patterns into functional (and professional) ones and was offered a most prestigious job opportunity with the company of her dreams.

This is just one example of how dysfunctional cycles can affect your work relationships. But what if your toxic and dysfunctional patterns affect your work performance, and ultimately your pay? Let's discuss Cassidy.

At face value, Cassidy is the most loving, attentive, aware, and social young lady. The other side that most people get a taste of frequently is the short-tempered, angry, undisciplined mouth, entitled young adult. Cassidy grew up in a house where the appearance of everything was more important than the reality of truth. If it looked good. If I deserved it, then I should have it; was what she was surrounded by her entire life. Her parents made Cassidy believe that since she was kind and social, she would get whatever she wanted. And if it didn't come, she would yell, cuss, and scream until you get it.

When we first met Cassidy, we saw the positive and loving attributes noted above. We only saw the other side as she described numerous amounts of incidents with other people that caused those unsightly behaviors to be on display. It was almost as if she was proud of having those moments until the shame of police reports, subpoenas, and lost jobs was the topic of conversation. Cassidy was clouded with a victim mentality and never connected her behaviors to the consequences she endured. Have you ever dealt with a person who believed the consequences that were given were always someone else's fault? That was Cassidy. It took us years of counsel to see a smidgen of self-awareness. And even with that minute amount of self-responsibility, she still made it appear to be a cause to her behaviors. What Cassidy didn't realize or have full understanding of is these cycles of dysfunction were passed down through former generations to include her parents. They still operate in them.

It's one thing when your behaviors affect relationships at work, but it is entirely different when those cycles of dysfunction cause you to get fired from every job. Cassidy would find great employment. She would develop genuine relationships with her co-workers and supervisors. The minute they did something she did not like, did not agree with, or didn't feel like doing, she would start to be disrespectful in tone and word choice. Most times Cassidy "felt" she had the right to react or act out based on her own entitled desires. Once those were unleased, she would get fired. After the firing, she would get upset, cry and seek out emergency assistance from those around her. The stories would always entail it was everyone else's fault. The company was horrible. The supervisor didn't know what they were doing. My co-workers lied on me. And the delusional reasons would go on and on. There would be very infrequent moments where Cassidy would say, "Yes, it was my attitude and mouth that got me fired." It would always be surrounded by what everyone else did.

What made things worse was, when Cassidy would explain herself or reasons for being fired to her parents, they would agree with her skewed perception of reality. They would even take it a step further to encourage taking legal action for illegal termination. Although Cassidy's terminations were definitely legal, and warranted, her parents' dysfunctional views on life causes Cassidy to remain in those cycles of dysfunction. It is like the social media phenomenon. No matter how wrong you are when posting an opinion, when someone likes your post, it gives the person posted a twisted confirmation that it is true and without error. Every time Cassidy's parents react in that way with her, it continues and strengthens the dysfunction.

We believe that when Cassidy sees the dysfunction that is operating in her life, which adversely affects her life and financial stability, she will flourish. It will be most challenging with her parents, especially if they want to remain in their cycles of dysfunction. Cassidy will have to assume a strong village that will hold her accountability and give her the support she will need. It will be difficult but not impossible to establish a new relationship with her parents in the midst of breaking these cycles of dysfunction. More importantly, it is crucial for her livelihood to develop functional ways of being, especially in the workplace.

Before tackling breaking cycles of dysfunction in the workplace, you must first deal with them in your current life. They only operate in the workplace because they are in operation outside of the workplace. The ability to manage conflict in a heathy manner may be a daunting and new task. However, it will take great maturity, discipline, and restraint to do such deeds. Learning to break cycles of dysfunction is necessary to obtain a well-rounded, full life that is producing in all areas. One area of dysfunction can have catastrophic consequences on multiple other areas of your life.

CHAPTER 4

RELATIONSHIPS/MARRIAGES

A re you the bag lady? Are you the never wanting to mature man? Do you know where that came from? What have you brought into a relationship and marriage that derived from cycles of dysfunction? These questions will be answered once you objectively look inward for the truth. So, this will be an introspective chapter. A chapter that will make you look hard at what you carry versus what/who you are. We will examine who we are personally in chapter 5. This chapter will discuss what you bring to relationships and/or marriages.

It may seem as if the Personality Traits chapter should come before this but most times, people are unaware of how toxic their personality traits are until they are in a relationship. It could be seen as backwards; however, we have seen it happen. Many times, being in covenant with people will cause you to look at areas of your individual self that you were unwilling to see before. Also, we can see how being connected in relationship may and will magnify dysfunctional cycles. We haven't researched enough of why dysfunctions are amplified in relationships, but we have a theory.

Our theory is that when people are in a relationship, rather romantically, platonically or in business, there are areas of ourselves we must openly hand over to other people. In turn, when you voluntarily hand over your vulnerabilities, fears, traumas, issues, etc., the other parties involved will react or respond with their own dysfunctions. This will become cataclysmic. Almost like two freight trains colliding. The good thing about this is, when there are two mature people colliding, they can rectify these issues in a healthy way and become better. However, when you don't have two mature people, or at least one objective person in the relationship, there can be trouble. Head on collisions typically don't end well. Nevertheless, healthy relationships and marriages should start with people willing to be open (at the appropriate time and space) about their problems and dysfunctions.

Dowrick pens,

> "Relationships get their best chance to succeed when they are most personal as well as most appreciative. That means resisting the temptation to generalize or to reduce someone to the sum of their faults and keeping communication going even in times of difficulty."[8]

Open communication about past and present cycles of dysfunction will be most beneficial in the partnership. That way both people are on board with assisting the other in times of difficulties. When this isn't present, or when either partner is unaware of their issues, dysfunctions incubate in the connection and bleeds through their relationship and others. Marriages see this most often.

When two people decide on committing their lives to one another forever, there comes a load of life experiences with it. Even when people don't suffer with trauma or abuse, there are inherited issues people have been imparted with that can affect their current relationships. For instance, we know siblings who were raised by parents who appeared to be very close and loving. The great patriarch of the family was in control of the family. The matriarch was a homemaker and took care of everything on the home front. They were heavily engaged with their children, church, and the community. On the outside looking in, it appeared this family had it all together and that the children were most disciplined, emotionally connected, well-being adults. However, when dissecting the realities of their rearing, it was exposed that their father only dealt with the boy children while their mother only dealt with the girl children. And what we mean by dealt with is, they were only disciplined and handled by the same sex parent. It may not appear to be dysfunctional at the onset. It becomes even more dysfunctional when these siblings have children of the opposite sex, and they have no emotional or parental connection with them.

There are plenty of reasons why the parents in this situation decided to rear their children in that way. But what has happened is, the siblings who are now parents will raise their children in the same oblivious dysfunction they grew up in. It is only at the moment the children (grandchildren to the patriarch) realize the dysfunction they were raised in and broke free from, that shines a light on what happened to their parents. In our experience, these exposures don't always end well, but they are necessary when breaking free from dysfunctional cycles. To further explain the dysfunction parents were raised in and imparted to their children goes like this.

The couple had 6 beautiful daughters. The parents were both raised in seemingly healthy marriages; however, the father was reared in the family explained above. The mother had her own difficulties growing up that was present in the family as well, but the focus of this example is on the dysfunction of the father. The father had ten total siblings, 5 boys and 5 girls. As stated above, his father disciplined the boys, the mother disciplined the girls. Neither parent was emotionally connected to their children. They didn't say I love you and were not affectionate. The child, we will call her Casey, was physically and verbally abused by her mother, and her father never stepped in. Casey did not understand why her father wasn't protective, or why he never physically disciplined her or the siblings. To be frank, Casey believed she had a great emotional relationship with her father until many years later it was unearthed as to be false. He was never available emotionally because he was not taught to feel emotion, regard emotion, be in touch with his emotion, nor share his emotion beyond a simple touch or hug. Casey brought this same emotionless energy into her own marriage. At first, she was not even aware of this emotionless dysfunction because she was and is very emotionally intelligent and affectionate. What made it clear to Casey that she was operating in dysfunction was when a close relative offered history to why the 10 siblings were emotionally absent. Once that was obvious, Casey saw how she would shut down in highly emotional situations. That in and of itself is not dysfunctional. It can very well be a trauma response. However, Casey was comfortable there. She could be in that emotionless state for hours, days, and even months. And to be very clear, this was not depression. The symptoms of depression can look very similar, but it was not that in this case.

Casey would go into these emotionless episodes when her feelings were hurt, when she felt slighted or disregarded. It would also show up after arguments with her spouse, or when she was despondent about something. Casey was operating in an inherited cycle of dysfunction her father grew up in. It was hard work for her to break it, but she was determined not to let it ruin her life or her marriage.

She would take note of those moments that initiated the emotionless response. Casey would evaluate what happened, how it made her feel, and why she was comfortable staying in that unemotional space. There was no benefit of staying there. It was just familiar. We introduced Casey to the steps that break cycles of dysfunction, and she got to work. It was challenging at first because it was so easy to go into an unemotional state. But when she was made aware of the reasons why she was doing it, Casey was even more determined to work the steps.

Acknowledging the cycles of dysfunction was step one. It came with a heap of emotions, no pun intended. This was a tough place to sit in. Not only did it make her recognize her own anger about the inherited dysfunction, but it also brought great clarity to how it possibly disconnected her from her husband and affected their children. Again, she was ignorant of the dysfunction she was operating in but at the same time fully operating in it. What a scary place to be. That's why it is vital to have emotionally healthy and discerning people part of your village. Someone should be able to spot dysfunction along with helping you through the healing process.

Confronting her father about this cycle of dysfunction almost set Casey's journey of healing back to square one. It came when an argument ensued about her feelings towards her father's absence of protection, and in a moment of fierce emotions, blurted out, "You need to get in tuned with your emotions! There are no feelings coming from you! Do you feel anything?" When her father heard this, he was livid. He wasn't upset because of what she asked him but rather that he was being confronted about not having emotions. In fact, he thought his unemotional stance or faux concern was actually conveying emotions. When evidence of our own behaviors is presented to us in the heat of an argument, most times it doesn't feel good. Can you imagine what could have happened if the father decided to actively listen to Casey, and then soberly assess the situation? It would have been tremendous for them both to walk through this journey of healing together. But in reality, people are not always ready to deal with the dysfunctions that so easily ruin their lives. Nonetheless, Casey realized it was a lost cause at that moment to continue the conversation although she sat in the realness of what it was. She pressed on with her journey of breaking cycles of dysfunction and has been successful with it.

The next couple we will discuss may seem or give the appearance of operating in an abusive nature. In our professional opinion, there was evidence of mental, psychological, and financial abuse amongst other things. Those areas of concern were examined thoroughly. And to make note again, the examples we give in this book are from real life situations and we personally know these people. They have been made aware of their contributions to this book. They have agreed to allow their stories to be told with anonymity to help other people break free from the cycles of dysfunction they've been consumed by.

The Gaines couple appeared to be picture perfect. In the eyes of all those they met, and who saw them on a regular basis. It was even verbally portrayed how "well" their relationship was based on everyone else. They, particularly the husband, made a conscious decision to verbalize how perfect things were, even when they were not. The most alarming was when he made note of being perfect in moments when his wife was visibly upset with him. Not once did he ever physically or verbally console her but made it very clear who was in charge, and that her feelings did not matter. The crazy part about that is, her feelings did not matter to him, but he then in turn told everyone how her feelings mattered. He did that with everything from what they would eat, what she would wear, and how she would conduct herself, and so on. It was a contradictory existence. Hypocritical at best, but he would never agree with that. His dysfunction was to show people he had great dominance. He learned that from watching his father have great dominance in the city they grew up in. However, the great dominance came with scandal, immoral behaviors, and some criminal interactions. Although she was clearly suffering from abuse, her own dysfunctional cycles were evident. She grew up in a family where the married women allowed their husbands to dominate them. Can you see how these two connected? It was okay for the women to stay in these cycles of dysfunctions especially if the men were taking care of them financially. At one point, we heard him say as long as he purchased her a new car, new hat or designer shoes, she would be fine with the poor treatment. And for whatever reason, she accepted it. It was almost a flex for her to walk around with designer shoes on knowing how and why she had them. Both of their inherited dysfunctions operated in tandem. They both benefited from it until it was done. What we mean by that is, once he realized he had dominated her entire early teenage years until her late 30s, there was no longer satisfaction. He had to move on to a new victim. Neither one decided to acknowledge and confront the cycles of dysfunction that were making them toxic as well as their marriage. This couple raised several kids during their marriage. At the end, the children sided with the dysfunctional cycles and poisonous lies their father spit out. It is not shocking to see how the children would side. If he came from dominance, they would follow suit and side with dominance.

The outcome of this situation is not ideal. It was not what could have happened. When you get two people who see their dysfunctions but benefit (in their minds) so greatly from it, they will choose to stay in it for one reason or another. The sad part is, they will both go into new situations with the same cycles of dysfunction. The kids will then have relationships in the same manner.

It is unfortunate to have seen so many couples operate in this same level of dysfunction. Even when they are unaware of the toxic generational patterns, at some point in their adult lives they should have a moment of mature clarity to see how their behaviors are impacting everything around them. In the event this is occurring with people you are familiar with, find a safe space to share with them your observations. If they are unwilling to listen and change, make your stance on what you are willing and not willing to accept, and move on.

Based on these two couple examples above, see below how the steps to break cycles of dysfunction are vital to their success. An example will be given for Casey and the Gaines. Since the Gaines did not agree to the steps, the examples will show what they should have done.

- Casey acknowledged the dysfunction she was operating in by realizing her own behaviors. When this step occurs without a third-party intervention, people are more apt to be successful. She was tired of how it made her feel, as well as how it made her husband feel. Although very difficult, Casey believed it would be more beneficial to tackle this toxic area in her life to stop it from further negative impact.

The Gaines could have acknowledged in a safe place at home the dysfunction they both were operating in. The conversation should not develop beyond that until there are safety measures in place. Based on their circumstances, it may go array quickly. In this space, we would recommend that the couple, at their own time, share with the other spouse THEIR observations of their own dysfunctions. This will not be the time that one spouse confronts the other spouse on what THEY are doing wrong.

- As in the scenario above, Casey confronted her father about the cycles of dysfunction she inherited. It did not go well. So, in this example, Casey should confront those in a healthy manner with support from loved ones what she has noticed in her life. If it is well received, she can then continue to share her own thoughts and then ask questions about the origin.

In our professional opinion, the only safe place for this conversation to happen after the initial step is in a license therapist office. The Gaines offer a unique situation that will need more support. If people are living in high levels of confusion, abuse, and dysfunction, anything can trigger violent or unwanted behaviors. Someone with skill and knowledge to handle these delicate situations will be crucial. We would also put a safety plan in place once they return home. Also, confrontation may begin with them before proceeding to outsiders. The couple will have to confront their own behaviors prior to confronting people who they believe are the causes of it.

- Renouncing will be necessary in both situations. Casey renounced her behavior and did not turn back. Her new actions were evident that she had taken the first two steps to get to this point.

The Gaines should have renounced their individual behaviors, as well as how those behaviors increased the dramatics of the relationship. Of course, this could only happen if both parties acknowledge their dysfunctions along with being ready for change.

- Finding new behaviors is a promising place to be. As stated previously, with Casey, she had acknowledged, confronted, and renounce all dysfunctional behaviors. She aslo developed new ways of thinking and being. The evidence was that she was stronger, and her marriage became strong and stable.

The only way to find new behaviors and positive creative ways to be is to go through the preceding steps. It would be counterproductive for the Gaines to jump to this step without the work needed beforehand. Like the saying goes, "you don't put a band aid on an oil leak"!

- Accountability is vital to the success in both examples. If Casey does not have strong accountability, it will be easy for her to fall back into the emotionless cycle. We deal with emotions every day of our lives, and in some cases, minute by minute, or hour by hour. If she does not have strong, consistent, and available accountability, it will be easy to relapse. And in her case, it will be easy to go there and stay. She will need someone to stay, "Get out!" of that place. Casey will benefit from accountability that will gently push her into expressing her feelings about situations versus having her own thoughts to herself. Most times with Casey, she was caught up in the trap of being comfortable without emotion. Her accountability team will have to be able to discern when she is falling into that state, and gently grab her by the hand and not allow it.

The Gaines, if they had desired, would benefit from an entire accountability team that includes license therapists, friends and other married couples who are healthy and know them well. The accountability team will have to be comfortable with confronting bad behavior immediately and maturely. The men on the team cannot try to one-up the husband, and the women cannot agree with the wife's dysfunction, nor give her counterproductive advice. The Gaines would have to give this team full disclosure with all areas of their lives, to include abuse in all forms. If they are unwilling to disclose the level of dysfunction and abuse, they are living in, the accountability team will be unsuccessful in their attempts to rectify dysfunctions that arise.

Carl Gustav Jung stated, "The meeting of two personalities is like the contact of two chemical substances: if there is any reaction, both are transformed."[9] Marriage is work even with the most healthy and aware people. And when people come together, there should be transformation although it takes work. The work will not be that complicated when people prepare for marriage and relationships beyond what they know. What we mean by that is, at the point two people are formally creating a relationship or marriage, they know each other up to that point. What they do not know is what happens after that moment. When each person is prepared to deal with or handle one another after that, the work becomes less complicated and more focused on the purpose of the union. The problems and issues that arise will be secondary to the purpose. They will be willing to quickly break free from whatever is coming against their relational destiny. Relationships and marriages are hard work. It doesn't have to be difficult to maneuver through if people are willing to look consciously, actively, and objectively inward to become better solely than jointly. What often happens is that people join the team before knowing what type of team member they are, and what they can offer effectively.

CHAPTER 5

PERSONALITY TRAITS

T here are hundreds and hundreds of documented personality traits. And there are distinct differences between positive and negative traits. Everyone comes equipped with some form of traits already inherited (genetics), but mostly our personalities derive from our environments and societal norms. Have you ever taken into consideration that those attributes developed from places of trauma and cycles of dysfunction? And that they may not be an accurate depiction of your personality? Let's discuss a personal revelation from Caitlyn about how she believes her personality developed, and then we will talk about Ally Brown.

Extroverted is a term used to describe types of personalities. It means, "an outgoing, overtly expressive person".[10] Introvert is the opposite of extrovert. Introvert is defined as, "a shy reticent person".[10] Defining these two terms will help in giving a complete understanding of how trauma colored Caitlyn's personality versus what was naturally/genetically developed. At first sight or initial interaction, people may think Caitlyn is extroverted. It happens because she is sociable, outgoing, and very expressive. She engages directly with people of all ages and backgrounds and finds it interesting to talk with random people. However, majority of the time, she is very introverted. She is not shy by any means but is very comfortable keeping to herself. There are times she enjoys not being social and not being talkative, but also loves being social and talkative.

There is a term that combines the two for more clarity. That term is ambivert. It is defined as, "a person whose personality has a balance of extrovert and introvert features".[10]

Again, Caitlyn can fall very comfortably into this category but if we look deeper, we can see the root cause of the introvert elements heavily represented because of the trauma she experienced.

Caitlyn was physically and verbally abused growing up. She even experienced it in her early adulthood. The abuse caused her to be mute, withdrawn, and recluse inside of the home. When she found herself in safe environments, free from her abuser, the outgoing, social, expressive person showed up. It was also a strong dichotomy of the two, and most people did not know both sides. There wasn't a literal switch that was turned off and on but the environments that were entered caused her to adjust drastically, especially when at home. Her friends, school, co-workers saw this social butterfly outside of the home, and her family saw a loner. Being alone became a form of protection rather than genetically developed personality traits. However, the opposite is true it became a natural environmentally developed personality trait. So, if you have the luxury of seeing Caitlyn in both places, outside and at home, you will see two sides of her personality which contributed to a cycle of dysfunction.

What we mean by that is, Caitlyn is aware that the introvert side of her personality derived from trauma and abuse. And instead of breaking it, she lived comfortably in it for many years. For the most part, Caitlyn was unaware of the dysfunctional aspects of her personality. She genuinely believed it was a part of who she was. Once the revelation came that this part of her was created because of the trauma she experienced, she worked hard at breaking it. Can you imagine how challenging it can be to become aware of, and diligently work at, correcting something that's been a part of you for many years? It was tough for Caitlyn but every day she is maturing in that area. When she feels like being in her shell and alone, she reminds herself that it is not a healthy place to be. That in fact, it is dysfunctional, and she is unwilling to return to that cycle. Later in this chapter, we will show through the steps how to break this dysfunctional personality trait using Caitlyn's example. Let's move on to Ally Brown.

Ally Brown is a beautifully vibrant young lady (remember names are changed to protect privacy). She was loving, kind, attentive, engaged, aware and very personable. On the flip side of that, she could be aggressive, assertive in the wrong settings, and overly emotional about things that didn't pertain to her. Ally had developed a sense that people were concerned about her when they weren't. During the height of this occurrence, Ally was determined to learn what had caused her to develop these dysfunctional traits and sought out wisdom to change them. It took a couple of years of painstaking recognition of those faulty areas but also great discipline to change them, which she did.

The dysfunctional personality trait that Ally developed was based on some areas she inherited from her family. What we mean by that is, Ally grew up in a family that dealt with alcohol, physical and verbal abuse. She learned early on that she would do the opposite of what she saw. If she saw her mother being verbally attacked by her drunken father, she was determined to be the aggressor when faced with a similar situation. Ally was quick to falsely assess a situation and react versus objectively assess a situation and respond. It had become her norm. It felt right to jump in and fight, even without knowing all the details. There was a dysfunctional tenacity in her to protect herself immediately. Ally had to learn that this was dysfunctional, and then to slow down. She had to renew her mind and ways of thinking. Her perception of most situations was colored by the lenses of her environment.

When Ally realized that the environment structured her dysfunctional traits, and that it was a cycle that plagued her family, she knew it would be necessary to change. However, the challenge was, would people like the new and improved Ally or would they resonate and remember the old? Ally had struggled at the beginning of this journey. When a personality trait has been with you for so long, or have become a part of who you are, it can be scary to change. Fear shows up when the unknown is present. There were many questions at the commencing, but it was vital in her processing through these major milestones. Once she broke through the fear, it was easier for her to accept the new person. The new challenge becomes not to fall back into the old but continue to press on with the new that is not dysfunctional in nature. Here is how both Caitlyn and Ally broke the cycle of dysfunction with their personalities.

- Caitlyn and Ally both started with acknowledging and exposing the cycles of dysfunction that plagued their personalities. Ally's accepting of the dysfunctional features was uncovered through counseling. Caitlyn became aware of hers through revelation. In these two examples the exposing was a vital beginning. There would be no second step if this wasn't tackled first. Both Ally and Caitlyn spent some time sitting in this step. It was difficult hearing the reality, and instead of moving forward quickly, they needed to stay in this place for a while. There was no need for a public declaration of what they discovered or the need to share. Although at times, there was a desire to share it with those who knew the old personality, quickly they realized the people who didn't accept the new benefited from their old dysfunctional ways. Boundaries were and are necessary in this stage to protect your heart from people's opinions about what should happen.

- Confronting yourself can feel strange in this situation. There is no need to go to the mirror and say, "your personality traits are dysfunctional" but if that's helpful to say it out loud, do it! Most people do not like to confront their own behaviors so this section may come with some difficulty. Having great support during this stage will help you to be sober in your assessment of the truth and encourage you to confront it. Ally found herself in a very vicarious position here. Acknowledging the dysfunction was not too hard; confronting it was. She thought confronting those familiar traits would cause her to lose family and friends. Caitlyn was already in a loner state, and she wasn't concerned about losing people rather than losing the fight to free herself.

- Abandon personality traits that are dysfunctional. Learn exactly what they are along with the behaviors that were associated with it. When you are in a healthy place, and people refer to you by the personality from the past, correct them. Ally had to do this a lot in the beginning. When she matured in her process, she realized how it wasn't needed to correct so often with words but rather show people with her newly found behavior. She had completely renounced the dysfunction and worked hard to correct the behaviors. Caitlyn didn't struggle with renouncing the dysfunctional traits but wrestled with the mental thoughts that took over when family and friends referenced the former dysfunctional ways. Maturing in this area is critical before moving to the next.

- In this section, it will be critical to fill those dysfunctional areas with Holy Spirit. Both Ally and Caitlyn are Believers of Jesus Christ. They knew that if they did not fill those dysfunctional areas with Him, it would have had an adverse effect on their healing. The standards they live by pulls them into a position that will glorify their God. Knowing that they were created in His image, and that nothing dysfunctional comes from God, it will be imperative to seek His guidance for their newfound image.

- One challenge they both dealt with when finding new and positive personality traits and being around their friends and family that knew them before, was to stay true to the new behaviors. It is easy to fall into the former habits.

- Caitlyn and Ally both have great accountability. They gave their spouses and close friends permission to hold them to their commitments of changing. There were rough spots with both during this time, but they persevered. Ally remembers being upset with her accountability partner when a family member was disrespectful towards her. The counsel she received was not to respond. Ally wanted to, and it made her upset with the advice. She had a moment, but got herself together and responded prudently, which in that case, was to not respond at all. Accountability for Caitlyn came from her spouse. When he saw her staying quiet and home more often, not speaking as much, he would make her plans to go out alone to her favorite store, as well as take her out on exciting dates. It lifted her spirits and renewed her sense of self.

Personality Traits Reflection Section

Sigmund Freud was a leading philosopher who did much research on personality, its etymology, and development. He was famous for creating the theory of psychosexual development which led to a Structural Model of Personality. Freud theorized that personality is developed over the course of childhood. It is the frame for how the personality functions and further develops as an adult. Freud documented that personality comes from the libido and it has three parts: the id, ego, and superego.[11]

The *id* is the raw, unorganized, inborn part of personality that is present at birth. It represents primitive drives related to hunger, sex, aggression, and irrational impulses. The id operates according to the *pleasure principle*, in which the goal is to maximize satisfaction and reduce tension.

The *ego* is the part of personality that is rational and reasonable. The ego acts as a buffer between the real world outside of us and the primitive id. The ego operates on the *reality principle*, in which instinctual energy is restrained in order to maintain the safety of the individual and help integrate the person into society.

Finally, Freud proposed that the *superego* represents a person's conscience, incorporating distinctions between right and wrong. It begins to develop around age 5 or 6 and is learned from an individual's parents, teachers, and other significant figures.[11]

Based on the findings of Freud, it is clear how dysfunction can find itself in either component of these aspects. What is even more obvious is that once you've bypassed the *id* and *ego*, the *superego* is where the dysfunction finds comfort and complacency. As an adolescent, dysfunctional personality traits are seared into your existence without the foreknowledge of what it can manifest into. This is a dangerous revelation to accept if there aren't any plans to help break cycles of dysfunction in those years rather than in adult hood. It has been stated publicly a million times that it takes about 21 days to break a bad habit and to form a new one. If we take this approach in helping people break cycles of dysfunction, we can begin preventative care with adolescents. We know that may sound extreme but follow for a few minutes.

If parents recognize their dysfunctional cycles, break them, and work at staying free from them, they will be able to identify it quickly in their children. Instead of minimizing certain behaviors as 'they are just kids', and investigate what is actually happening, the parents would be able to adjust those behaviors in a shorter time span. As adults, especially those in the later years of life, who have been connected with their dysfunction for many generations may find it more difficult to do away with certain behaviors, and for a myriad of reasons. If you've had an addiction to illegal substances for 40 years, it may take more time to be sober than someone who was addicted for 1 year. When you pick up the correlation between this example, you can see how effective it would be to stir the personalities of adolescents into positive ones, rather than give light and focus on the negative ones. Most times, parents ignore the red flags of behaviors of their children believing they will grow out of it. What we have seen is that these children grow into it. They grow into having horrible attitudes and unpleasurable behaviors instead of growing out them. It is our responsibility as parents to rear children to the best of our abilities so they will be productive citizens. If parents are unwilling to acknowledge and confront dysfunctional personality traits in their own lives, how can they then handle it with children? Nonetheless, if you agree with Freud's position on the development of personality traits or not, it is understood that developing personalities is a multifaceted concept. There may be genetics, environments or traumas that come into play when ciphering through someone's personality. At best, it is vital to understand what is operating when seeing these dysfunctional traits.

With the information that has been presented thus far it is safe to assume that dysfunctional behaviors can begin where there is a need/desire or lack of. To explain this finding, we were watching another documentary on a popular app. It was discussing the details of robberies that happened in Hollywood, California. This documentary confirmed that the unhealthy need for fame, status and friendships, which is dysfunctional, can lead to a criminal enterprise.

Can you see how the dysfunctional wants manifested into dysfunctional behaviors?

Once the initial perverted thoughts entered in, or the dysfunctional behaviors emerged, it then became a planned-out flaw, distorted goal. This is precisely how dysfunctional cycles begin and get passed on to subsequent generations if not taken care of once recognized. Have you ever taken into consideration that the dysfunctional cycle you are operating in has nothing to do with you? It has nothing to do with your personality traits, your attributes, or anything you desire to be. It somehow intrusively enters in and now you have been consumed by this unhealthy invisible pattern. We believe that was the issue with one of the characters in the documentary. They were reared in a family that only wanted fame, fortune, and status, and would do anything to get it done. The parents passed those same unhealthy desire to their children. Although the parents did not do anything criminal or illegal to gain the status, they were oblivious that their children may pick up those dysfunctional ways and step it up a few notches. So when

the dysfunctional personality traits become dysfunctional behaviors, that have criminal consequences, it has past time to look at the root causes. But as in this documentary, the way the character explains how and why he did things in the past, there is still a sense of pride and excitement that exudes when discussing the criminal details. It is fair to assess that those rooted dysfunctional traits and desires are still present. If not dealt with, this character will then pass on to following generations. That's when you will hear, "they act just like their father!"

Have you ever heard this expression; the apple doesn't fall too far from the tree? Did it resonate with you? Or did it make you feel angry and want to be disassociated from the apple tree? In most instances, this is a very true statement unless you work hard at breaking that connection. And it is definitely not a rule, but it is something that occurs often within families. There must be intentionality in order to remove yourself from dysfunctional cycles, especially if they are familiar and family driven. You don't have to be associated with toxic, dysfunctional behaviors, even when they are family members.

When you have specific unhealthy mentalities, dysfunctional behaviors typically follow. Mother worked 2 and 3 jobs because she had a poverty mentality or didn't want to be faced with poverty, so she overworked. Now you have a son who is highly educated, competent, healthy, and successful at one job also working 2-3 jobs because that's the dysfunctional cycle he saw growing up. Being highly educated and qualified does not exempt you from dysfunctional cycles if they go unacknowledged.

CHAPTER (6)

HOW TO BREAK CYCLES

I f you know something is bad for you, would you continue to do it? If yes, why? If no, do you have the wherewithal or discipline to break it? How many people do you know who've suffered from addiction, and they shared with you how hard it was to break? There are countless reasons, excuses, obstacles, hinderances, and the alike that keep people from stopping the addiction. What if part of the problem was that people were unaware that there was an addiction or problem? How can you be responsible to break something if you are unaware that it exists? This chapter will dive into identifying and understanding dysfunctional cycles, possible causes, impacts, and if you are ready to change. Understanding dysfunctional cycles will help you process how to break them.

While researching how cycles develop and persist, we stumbled across an article written by Harrison Wein, PhD titled, "Breaking Bad Habits: Why It's So Hard to Change" and in this article he quoted research from Dr. Nora Volkow, the director of the News In Health National Institute on Drug Abuse.[12] Her study focuses on why people have habits whether good or bad and how does the biology of these people affect those routines. Wein quotes Volkow by saying,

> "Habits play an important role in our health,"…"Understanding the biology of how we develop routines that may be harmful to us, and how to break those routines and embrace new ones, could help us change our lifestyles and adopt healthier behaviors."[12]

> Habits can arise through repetition. They are a normal part of life and are often helpful. "We wake up every morning, shower, comb our hair or brush our teeth without being aware of it," …. We can drive along familiar routes on mental autopilot without really thinking about the directions. "When behaviors become automatic, it gives us an advantage, because the brain does not have to use conscious thought to perform the activity," …. This frees up our brains to focus on different things.[12]

> Habits can also develop when good or enjoyable events trigger the brain's "reward" centers. This can set up potentially harmful routines, such as overeating, smoking, drug or alcohol abuse, gambling and even compulsive use of computers and social media.[12]

These possibly toxic cycles can also come in the form of behaviors, mentalities, thoughts, attitudes, and beliefs from generations of family members. That is why it's important to be soberly aware of what is going on in your life holistically. Sometimes it's not just good enough to know you are a good person, or educated, or compassionate. You have to be so in tune with the negative aspects of your life, behaviors, etc. so you can break cycles of dysfunctions before they become so habitual that it is challenging to break through them. Wein reported, "Enjoyable behaviors can prompt your brain to release a chemical called dopamine."[12] It has not been researched enough to be definitive, but all enjoyable behaviors do not have to necessarily be good behaviors for dopamine to release. Steve Calechman, a contributor at Harvard Health Publishing stated in the article, "How to Break a Bad Habit",

> "Often, habits that don't benefit us still feel good, since the brain releases dopamine. It does this with anything that helps us as a species to survive, like eating or sex. Avoiding change qualifies as survival, and we get rewarded (albeit temporarily), so we keep reverting every time."[13]

There is a strong possibility that criminal activity can also be 'enjoyable' to the brain in order for dopamine to distribute throughout the body. It is safe to assume that this is exactly what happens. Why would people continue to knowingly do dangerous and criminal behavior if there were no physical rewards? Even with dysfunctional attitudes, beliefs, and behaviors; there are rewards.

We were watching a show about parenting, and this mother stated her 6-year-old daughter thrives on negative reinforcement. To be very clear, we do not agree with that statement and gagged when she said it out loud on national television. Nonetheless, the little girl was a certified genius. She was homeschooled by her mother, and absolutely disliked doing schoolwork. All she wanted to do was play with her toys. She was also gifted at playing several different instruments along with her academic success. The mother used inappropriate name calling that would get the child's attention, and then she would reluctantly complete her task. We're not certain if the dopamine was released in the child's brain but it was definitely a sick reward for her mother. She was the one who thrived on her daughter's accomplishments. The little girl only wanted to be a kid, and play. Although she enjoyed doing schoolwork, and was excited when her answers were correct, the mother flourished on the dysfunctional aspect of getting her to that point and could careless how it could negatively affect her daughter's well-being. This caused a strain in the relationship. The daughter didn't want anything to do with her mother. It was difficult for the mother to come to terms with the fact that she forced the daughter's academic schedule and outside of that, wanted to be left alone. It was a dysfunctional cause and effect that was initiated by her mother's need to have a certified genius child.

What causes dysfunctional cycles and behaviors? Based on what was documented above, there could be a reward granted for those actions which cause people to continue with them. That is one liable answer when we deal with dysfunctional patterns. Granted, people may be totally unaware of their dysfunctional ways, and have no ability to change. But even with that, there is still some type of gain that pleases the senses of the person operating in them. Nevertheless, let's start from the beginning with childhood. This will give us a well-rounded view of how these cycles develop, the causes, even when they had nothing to do with the person functioning in them.

Corneila Schneck writes something important dealing with the inner child and how negative patterns from childhood could be a cause in forming bad habits.[14] In our opinion, Schneck is accurate in her assessment of how unsightly behaviors began in early childhood but to take it a step further, we can say that these behaviors could have, and most likely began with their parent having that same issue. For example, if there is a mother who has a distorted body image. Her issues with her own body image will consume her speech when speaking to her daughter. Now unconsciously, the daughter is hypersensitive about body image as an adolescent. If the mother had taken care of her dysfunctional view of her body, she would have consciously and unconsciously given her daughter a healthy view of her own body. What caused the mother to have a distorted view of her own body could be multifaceted. She could have been molested, sexually assaulted, or inherited the same perceptions from her mother. Unless there is intensive digging and great revelation, it can be challenging to pinpoint the exact entrance wound. Schenk pens,

> As children we created an image of ourselves through key emotional experiences. In line with this, we have developed strategies for being loved by parents. We paid for this with the child's pain, which was not allowed to develop according to its nature. These inhibiting experiences are still present in our adult lives. If a situation reminds us of an unresolved conflict from childhood, it emerges in the form of negative thought patterns such as: "I don't belong", " I have to adapt", "I can't do it", "I'm worthless" or "Nobody loves me". The pain associated with it can still be so alive in an adult that he does not feel cared for and at home in his life.[15]

Key emotional experiences do not have to be our own. Children can join into the dysfunctional emotional experiences with a parent and adopt their slanted view of something. This reminds me of the quote made by Nelson Mandela in "A Long Walk to Freedom",

> "No one is born hating another person because of the color of his skin, or his background, or his religion. People must learn to hate, and if they can learn to hate, they can be taught to love,

for love comes more naturally to the human heart than its opposite."[15]

Children are not born with dysfunction. They have learned dysfunction. Whatever they have picked up from previous generations is operating in their current lives. Again, it was not their own dysfunctional cycle, it was passed down. And this is one of the causes to why adults operate in dysfunctional cycles. If you take a sober assessment of your own life, you can look back and see what dysfunctional views, behaviors, attitudes, and ways of doing things that you are operating in that were picked up. Root causes can be a variety of different things, traumas, abuse, mishandlings, and lies. How many fabricated stories do we repeat without understanding the truth of what happened? This is the same with behaviors. We can function in cycles that were not started in truth or positivity. David T. Courtwright states that the longer you operate in an addiction or habitual pattern, it's likened to "…drops of dye spreading on a taut sheet."[16] It will begin small, and then cover more areas. He further states, "The earlier children and adolescents experience an addictive substance or pastime, the likelier they are to retain, even when abstaining, a powerful emotional memory of the behavior that once made them feel so good".[16] Who would want to stop something that makes them feel good, especially after experiencing it for so many years. This is impactful on the person and those around them.

From the authors of, "Bad Habits in Children and their Impact on Oral Health and Development of Teeth, "A habit is a repetitive action that is performed automatically or spontaneously".[17] The dentist involved in authoring this article argued and proved that dysfunctional cycles impacted the oral health of children. This can also be said of adults. If we are consistent in wrong dental habits as children, and not corrected, it will be present in adulthood. It was further stated,

> "Bad habit is defined as stereotypical repetitions of the functions of the mastication system, which differ qualitatively and quantitatively from their physiological functions. Bad habits usually happen quietly so that children do not realize that they often do this. The habit is initially carried out in a conscious state, but repetition results in decreased awareness and motor response. Eventually the habit is fully formed and becomes part of the mind's routine, making it more difficult to get rid of."[17]

Quiet dysfunction becomes loud dysfunction. And then consistent cycles of dysfunction. Just sit in that for a moment. That quote is a lot to take in. What a powerful statement to make, "Bad habits usually happen quietly..."[17] The impact of something beginning and operating quietly to manifesting publicly and loudly is scary. There are no other words to fit this moment. It is scary to deal with an involuntary invisible thing that is tangible. If this is not a reason to jump start your change today, then you don't want it to happen. You have been complicit in your own dysfunction at this point. There is no longer an excuse to pass fault to another person, although it would be an accurate placement. When you have discovered dysfunctional aspects of your life, it is now your responsibility to change them! So why change? What's in it for you? What's in it for those around you?

Wein stated, "Bad habits may be hard to change but it can be done."[12] We couldn't agree with him more. It will take work and discipline, but it is doable. The reason behind your necessary change is also very important. Calechman wrote, "...before you try to change a habit, it's fundamental to identify *why* you want to change. When the reason is more personal…you have a stronger motivation and a reminder to refer back to during struggles".[13] Holding on to your reason or reasons throughout this process is crucial for your success.

It has been widely researched that when people are motivated and ready to change, their outcome of success is more visible. There is no reason to begin the steps of changing if there is nothing to motivate your process. It is vital that your reason(s) rest heavily on your own desire to change versus the focus being on someone else's happiness. Ultimately the healing is for yourself and everyone around you will benefit from the results. Wood, Esplin, Hatch, Dodini, Braithwaite, and Ogles, studied several people dealing with pornography addiction and concluded that most of the participants who successfully completed treatment wanted to change.[18] They further described that the reasons to get help spanned from religion, social norms, relationships, partnerships, and stigmas that affected their well-being.[18] Although it is essential to have a reason to change, readiness to change trumps reasons. Because when, not if, you are faced with a situation that provokes you to resort back to holding behaviors, your readiness to change will be the force to not go back. The discipline to ready yourself, hold true to those convictions, stay with the change, and tangibly see the outcomes becomes valuable to the person breaking cycles of dysfunction.

Here is how you break cycles of dysfunction. The steps include:

- Acknowledge/Expose

- Confront

- Renounce

- Deliverance/Escape (Stop what you are doing)

- Replace/Change

- Find/Create New Behaviors

- Accountability

➤ Acknowledge is a verb that means to accept or admit the existence or truth of [something]. Expose is a verb defined to make (something) visible by uncovering it, or true, objectionable nature of (someone or something).

Acknowledging and/or exposing the cycle(s) of dysfunction is the first step. There can be no process, journey or healing without this stage. It would be foolish to think someone can correct a mistake they have made without recognizing the mistake. It may seem simple, but in some cases, this step may be the hardest to do. Most people become uncomfortable when other people expose their shortcomings, how much more challenging is it to acknowledge your own (and how it affected other people). Once you have tackled that hurdle, admitting that you are operating in dysfunction is a natural place to begin.

Throughout this book there have been examples given on how to handle this phase. If none of those examples resonate with you, here is how you can acknowledge and expose your dysfunction.

I, insert name here , have been dealing with insert dysfunctions here . And I am acknowledging and exposing the cycles of dysfunction operating in my life.

Recite this line as many times as necessary. Include all forms of dysfunctions, as well as in what ways it has affected your life. Also list the losses. For example,

I, insert name here , have been dealing with insert dysfunctions here . It has affected, areas affected . I have lost enter losses . I am acknowledging and exposing the cycles of dysfunction operating in my life.

If you would like to expose more details of your cycles of dysfunction, this is also a good place to do it.

I, insert name here , have been dealing with insert dysfunctions here , for insert how many years. The dysfunctions began with root (i.e my mother) . And I am acknowledging and exposing the cycles of dysfunction operating in my life.

This is how it will read.

I, Julia , have been dealing with being angry and aggressive, for 25 years. The anger and aggression began with my mother. I never had the problem. She shared with me through stories and behaviors to act this way. I have lost friendships, romantic relationships, and jobs. My life has been on hold because I cannot proceed from the anger, she instilled in me. I am acknowledging and exposing the angry and aggressive cycles of dysfunction that have operated in my life since childhood.

➢ Confront is a verb defined as meet[ing] (someone) face to face with hostile or argumentative intent. We do not recommend or suggest that this confrontation be hostile or argumentative. Healthy confrontation is necessary. It is important. Even if you confront yourself about the behaviors. Setting the stage for healthy confrontation looks like this.

I,   insert name here   , will no longer deal with   insert dysfunctions here   . I will not let   dysfunctions   keep me from fulfilling my purpose and destiny. I will not let   dysfunctions   stop me from moving forward in life. I will not let   dysfunctions   bleed onto my family or children. It stops with me. It stops now!

Feel free to customize this sentence to fit your situation. It does not have to read line for line. However, making sure the dysfunctions are entered correctly along with emphasis on what you will not continue to allow.

➢ Renounce is to formally declare one's abandonment of (a claim, right, or possession).

I,   insert name here   , renounce   insert dysfunctions here   . I (publicly/privately) refuse to abide by these   dysfunctions   behaviors. From this day forward, I will no longer be associated with the cycles of dysfunction that have plagued my life.

➢ Deliverance/Escape (Stop what you are doing). The action of being rescued or set free is the definition of deliverance. Escape is to break free from confinement or control.

I,___insert name here___, will be set freed from the confines of ___insert dysfunctions here___. I will no longer allow ___dysfunctions___ to control my thoughts and behaviors. I will remain free from previous actions, mindsets, and behaviors. If for any moment I resort back to old ways, I will press harder onto the reasons why it is important for me to stay free.

➤ Replace/Change: Take the place of something and make (someone or something) different; alter or modify. If you are a believer of Jesus Christ and are submitted to His standards, this and the subsequent section will allow you to replace old dysfunctional behaviors with the truth of who He is. This will also allow you to find new behaviors, mindsets, and hobbies in Him.

I,___insert name here___, change the former ___insert dysfunctions here___ behaviors and replace them with ___desired behaviors___. I will not pressure myself to replace and change old ways quickly. I will take my time and focus on small steps moving forward. I will not let anyone dictate how slow or fast I go. I will not let anyone manipulate me into going back to the old dysfunctional behaviors.

➤ Find/Create New Behaviors. Discovering new positive and socially acceptable behaviors will be vital after you have decided to replace and change them. These two sections (one above) will work in tandem.

I,___insert name here___, will find and/or create new behaviors for previously dysfunctional patterns. Those new behaviors will include _____list_____. I will work on these for the next _____insert time frame_____.

> Accountability: the fact of condition of being accountable; responsibility.

I,___insert name here___, will acquire a team of accountability partners for this journey of breaking cycles of dysfunction. My team will consist of _____name_____ as the lead partner. _____name_____ will be allowed to have name and contact information for the rest of my team. The other members of the team are: _____names_____. I will meet (via in-person, facetime, or phone) with _____name/leader_____, once a week until there is significant change. Once a month, I will meet with the entire team (via in-person, facetime, or phone) to discuss progress and areas of improvement. The frequency of subsequent meetings will be determined by _____name/leader_____. This team has permission to hold me accountable in all situations pertaining to former cycles of dysfunction, as well as with new behaviors. In the event there are discrepancies with former and new behaviors, meetings will be documented to assure accuracy of decisions made. It is my responsibility to effectively communicate with my team in areas I am struggling in. They will have full disclosure of my temptations and areas of concerns. I will submit myself to their wisdom and help.

It is worth knowing that anytime during this breaking cycles journey, there may be times a person revisits a stage they were once at. This is not indicative of failure. It is evidence that a person is working the system. The only true failure is if a person quits and never returns. Take your time with these stages. It is not a sprint. It is a marathon. It will take time, energy, effort, and discipline. It is work! It is also very rewarding!

CHAPTER (7)

HOW TO MANAGE DYSFUNCTIONAL PEOPLE (FUNCTIONAL BALANCE)

S o, you have been intently reading through each chapter. Learning and yielding to the process of breaking cycles of dysfunction. Then you get to a place where you are fully aware of the work you've done and see the obvious dysfunctional behaviors constantly around you. What do you do? How do you navigate through this public part of the process? These questions are valid, and typically very apparent at this point in the juncture. It is critical to both be aware of and have a plan to conquer these moments where you are faced with people or family in your former dysfunction, while they sit comfortably in their current dysfunction. It is not your job to strong arm them into believing what you now know was dysfunction. However, you can allow your changed behaviors and new life to speak for you without a fight. Let your renewed mind provoke them to want to change their lives too. Nevertheless, no matter how far you've come into this process, or how long you've been healthy, it is still a realistic fear on how to manage the dysfunctional people and family around you.

We have been teaching people for years this stance, "If you don't manage your expectations, you will manage your disappointments." Managing expectations comes with open communication and discussion on what you expect from someone, a relationship, or partnership. If these things are not communicated in the beginning, you will find yourself managing the disappointments. And to be clear, managing disappointments does not mean regurgitating and rehearsing bad situations. It means that when you experience a situation or behavior that you didn't expect, or discuss, now you are dealing with the heartache and pain from what you failed to speak about initially. So, the rules of engagement with this are to think about, write down, and thoroughly discuss your expectations from yourself, those around you, as well as your accountability team. However, what is most important to learn in this chapter is how to manage dysfunctional people when: 1. You have broken free from it, but they have decided to stay in their dysfunction and, 2. What is a healthy and unhealthy way of dealing with dysfunctional people.

Our desire in this chapter is to teach you functional balance. The dichotomy between being passive and an accessory to their dysfunction to standing bold and confident in freedom! Let's begin with number 1.

1. They have decided to stay in their dysfunction.

As stated in previous chapters, it is not your responsibility to strong arm or violently persuade people to follow you in breaking cycles of dysfunction. Yes, we want to see all people living a healthy, stable, dysfunctional free life, however, you cannot force someone to do so. When people have decided in one way or another to stay in their dysfunction, you have to set boundaries. Let me be clear, BOUNDARIES, BOUNDARIES, BOUNDARIES, are necessary! They are vital to your process as well as your mental health. You cannot allow dysfunctional attitudes and behaviors to make you relapse. It is also very important to be aware that people, especially family members and close friends will try to guilt trip you into falling back. That is why it is crucial to set up healthy boundaries.

Boundaries can include but not limited to:

A. Stopping all communication!

B. Restricting access to you. In person and through social media.

C. If the first two are not possible, limit your time and exposure to those people.

D. If you feel yourself getting into an old place with former behaviors or attitudes, remove yourself immediately and call an accountability partner.

E. When you notice the dysfunctional person trying to encourage you to go backwards, revisit steps A and B.

2. What is a healthy and unhealthy way of dealing with dysfunctional people?

It is safe to assume that when people are engulfed in dysfunction, their meter for healthy boundaries can be off. When one deems something healthy, unhealthy, it will cause tremendous problems. It's vital for people to understand what is healthy and unhealthy before applying these suggestions.

Example A: A healthy way of dealing with someone dysfunctional is having a conversation about your boundaries and decision to stop all communication until further notice. The unhealthy way of handling the situation is to ignore them. Leaving people without a conversation is cowardice. We understand people may not be mature enough to handle these levels of communication, however, it is your responsibility to announce your departure. Don't leave people in the dark about what you are doing regarding them.

Example B: Understanding that you cannot hang out with people who are operating in their own dysfunction or the same dysfunction you have just been freed from. The unhealthy way to approach this is to ignorantly believe you will be fine in the midst of this dysfunction and not feel tempted to indulge. Liken this example to a former alcoholic bar hopping with friends. At some point, they will feel the temptation to drink whether they indulge or not. In this stage of your journey, even feeling tempted can have catastrophic consequences.

There can be a thousand different examples of healthy and unhealthy ways of handling situations. The most important thing to know is the difference between the two and behave appropriately. If in doubt always seek guidance from your accountability team. Having a plan is the best way to be successful at all times.

Your plan to have functional balance must include a script and a plan. We find it beneficial to have both so that you aren't left not knowing what to do in the moment. For example, we had a friend leaving a job shortly after being hired. The trauma and dysfunction she experienced in life caused her to feel she owed everyone an explanation of her decisions. It was exhausting for her to live in, always explaining why or how she was doing something. It wasn't until we counseled her that she realized the dysfunctional and exhausting behaviors. What we suggested included having a script ready. To stand boldly on it, and to not offer anything after that other than a smile and salutation. The script stated something similar to this, "I've enjoyed my time here, but I have a new assignment elsewhere." When co-workers, or other employees would ask why she was leaving so abruptly, that was her response. Instead of having a 45-minute conversation with every single person, laced with high emotions and guilt, this was her way of setting boundaries with herself, as well as those who expected a detailed explanation from her. She learned to handle dysfunctional and intrusive people properly and strongly. And without compromising her progress in her own journey of healing.

CHAPTER 8

HOW NOT TO "MANAGE" DYSFUNCTION

This entire book has been about how to break cycles of dysfunction, and what it looks like in your own family, your personality, at work, in relationships and so on. We also instruct through the chapters of this book how to walk out the journey of healing with steps to ensure success. These steps include scripts to use, ways to pick out a strong accountability team, and how to know the difference between healthy and unhealthy boundaries. This chapter will teach you how NOT to manage dysfunction!

The definition of manage is to be in charge of; administer; run. In this case, we do not want to be in charge of your dysfunction or anyone else's. Just like in Chapter 7, you were taught to have healthy boundaries, you need to understand in this chapter to not feel obligated to handle another person's dysfunctional ways. You may try to convince yourself that it will be helpful or keep the peace. It's a false sense of peace. It will be exhausting, and it won't end well.

A friend of ours was speaking to me about an interpretation of a dream. He was unaware at the time the final touches were being made on this book. He was giving instructions on how to handle dysfunctional people, especially if they are in some form of authority over you. When he said it, we knew immediately that we had to add it to this book. Andrew Duncan of Nova Scotia, Canada said, "Be at peace inside the dysfunction [of other people]. Don't get wrapped up in partaking of the dysfunction. Don't allow yourself to be held accountable [for their] dysfunction, and don't become intertwined in it."

You do not manage dysfunction by allowing the dysfunction around you to consume you. It is necessary to know that when dealing with dysfunctional people or systems, you must be fully aware of what is occurring. You also have to be cognizant not to fall victim to it. Dysfunction cannot be managed, especially if you were once an active participant in the dysfunction. You either fully operate in dysfunction, or you do not. There should not be any gray areas with this. It is simply black and white. Hot or cold. You have to choose one or the other.

A practical explanation on how NOT to manage dysfunction will look like this, and this example has been mentioned before but it's such a great illustration. When a former alcoholic believes they can manage their sobriety by going to bars every night. Maintaining sobriety or managing sobriety should not come with being placed in the very space connected to alcoholism. That is how one should NOT manage their sobriety. The same is true for people recovering from cycles of dysfunction. You should not surround yourself with the same or new dysfunctional people believing your recovery will be strong and stable. It is delusional to believe you can keep the cycles of dysfunction at bay while being in midst of the ones who taught you how to be dysfunctional or with people who do not believe their behaviors are dysfunctional. It is okay to have boundaries. You are not obligated to be in the company of dysfunctional people or systems as a tangible sign that you are strong enough to withstand it. Do not put yourself in compromising situations that may cause you to revert to what you stepped out of. And do not allow people who are operating dysfunctionally, make you feel less than when you decide to do something different!

Remember, breaking cycles of dysfunction is an ongoing journey. It is an inward work that manifests outwardly. It will be tangible if you do the work. You should see change in every area of your life once you have decided to tackle those dysfunctional cycles.

Continue to be intentional about breaking cycles of dysfunction by reading and completing the rest of the book. Chapter 9 will give you hashtags from years of thought on breaking cycles of dysfunction. By reading them, you may find one or many that resonate with your life. Let that fuel you to pursue change! In Chapter 10, you'll be able to acknowledge and expose cycles of dysfunction in your life, write out a plan, and begin your journey!

CHAPTER 9

HASHTAGS

This chapter is a collection of thoughts we have shared throughout the past 3 years on social media. They came from moments of revelation, clarity, or noticing someone dealing with a dysfunctional cycle. Feel free to go on social media and put in the hashtag #Breakingthecyclesofdysfunction and see what comes up.

The inability to recognize Dysfunctional behaviors will keep you stuck in unhealthy cycles. #BreakingtheCyclesofDsyfunction

Dysfunction starts in your mind. Your thoughts will drive the behavior. #BreakingtheCyclesofDsyfunction

By NOT dealing with the Trauma, you still deal with it. It's time to be free. #BreakingtheCyclesofDsyfunction

Thought: Stop normalizing dysfunction and calling it discipline. #Breakingthecyclesofdsyfunction

Dysfunction starts in your mind. Your thoughts will drive the behavior. #BreakingtheCyclesofDsyfunction

You can't manipulate people and call it God!! #BreakingtheCyclesofDsyfunction

The inability to recognize Dysfunctional behaviors will keep you stuck in unhealthy cycles. #BreakingtheCyclesofDsyfunction

Those who were exposed to high levels of trauma are at a greater risk of being deceived. It's time to be free. #BreakingtheCyclesofDsyfunction

Attention seeking behavior is NOT of God.#BreakingtheCyclesofDsyfunction

A spirit of delusion has swept over on people, and it is tremendous. People are so arrogant in their delusion that they believe their own delusion!

#Theydrinktheirownkoolaid

#breakingthecyclesofdysfunction

It is very dysfunctional to think that you can ignore the pain of betrayal and keep going as if nothing happened. Assess the pain, bandage your wounds and Heal. #Itstimetoheal #BreakingtheCyclesofDysfunction

The emotions and feelings that you have suppressed and kept quiet will eventually begin to YELL. #Talkaboutit #BreakingtheCyclesofDysfunction

The spirit of pride, arrogance, and hatred all leads to death! They are murderous spirits. Be careful of what you say. Be mindful of what you come into agreement with because there is true believer's praying for God's protection over who you think ain't (I said it!) worthy!! And the fight will be against anyone who said it or came into agreement with it. #Imreadytofight #itstimeforarevolution #breakingthecyclesofdysfunction

Sometimes people don't want to understand or say they don't understand because it doesn't fit into the preconceived, made-up or lie they have in their own head.

#breakingthecyclesofdysfunction

Demonic cycles will stay in rotation so as long as you keep repeating the things that keep you bound. It's time to be free. #BreakingtheCyclesofDysfunction

Most Dysfunctional people can't recognize the Dysfunctional behaviors within themselves. #breakingthecyclesofdysfunction

After a certain age, being messy is a sign of misery. #breakingcyclesofdysfunction

Refuse to inherit dysfunction. #breakingcyclesofdysfunction

When you defend the dysfunctional. You have also been bewitched by the dysfunction!

#breakingthecyclesofdysfunction

The Lord has stripped your idols and YOU have run back to them! #breakingthecyclesofdysfunction

People who exalt themselves above God, correction, repentance, and humility are often in dysfunction. Who you are submitted too can help shed light on this.

#breakingthecyclesofdysfunction

If you are tied to/connected to the dead...how can you not smell like rotten flesh?

#breakingthecyclesofdysfunction

CHAPTER 10

THE PLAN

E xam yourself. Do it soberly. What dysfunctional cycles do you see in your life or family? In this section of the book, use these pages to acknowledge and expose those dysfunctional cycles, write out a plan/steps to break them, find new behaviors, attitudes, or ways of being using the scripts in chapter 6.

Then in the final section of this book, attach your accountability plan. We believe it is vital to the success of any plan is to write it out. Visibly seeing things, in our opinion, makes them real. It also becomes evidence of the former behaviors becoming new, with tangible change.

Feel free to write this section out on your own paper or in your journal. There is also a Breaking Cycles of Dysfunction Workbook available to purchase. It is complete with each section, and areas to write down your plan.

Sections:

➢ Dysfunctional cycles

➢ Root causes of dysfunctional cycles

➢ Areas, these dysfunctional cycle have impacted

➢ Steps and plans to break them

➢ New behaviors, attitudes, mindsets

➢ Accountability plan

➢ Weekly/Monthly/Yearly Follow-up

NOTES

1. https://www.cdc.gov/nchs/fastats/marriage-divorce.htm

2. https://www.statista.com/statistics/191231/reported-aggravated-assault-rate-in-the-us-since-1990/

3. Berlinger, J., Doran, J., Kamen, J., Isaacson, J., & Samantha Grogin. 2023. *Madoff: The Monster of Wall Street* [TV Series]. Netflix. https://www.netflix.com/title/81466159

4. Segeren, M., Fassaert, T., de Wit, M. et al. Constellations of youth criminogenic factors associated with young adult violent criminal behavior. Crime Sci 9, 2 (2020). https://doi.org/10.1186/s40163-020-0111-2

5. Kelly, W., Macy, T.S., & Daniel P. Mears.Juvenile Referrals in Texas: An Assessment of Criminogenic Needs and the Gap Between Needs and Services. *The Prison Journal* Volume: 85 Issue: 4 Dated: December 2005 Pages: 467-489

6. United States number of working people.

7. Dolman, M. (2023, January 5). How does the EEOC Identify a Hostile Work Environment?. https://www.dolmanlaw.com/blog/eeoc-identify-hostile-work-environment/

8. Dowrick. (2004). *Free Thinking On Happiness, Emotional Intelligence, Relationships, Power and Spirit.* Allen & Unwin.

9. Carl Gustav Jung quote online

10. https://www.dictionary.com/

11. Feldman. (2010). *Development across the life span* (Sixth edition.). Prentice Hall.

12. Wein, Harrison (2012, January). *Breaking Bad Habits: Why It's So Hard to Change* News In Health National Institute.

13. Calechman,S. (2022, May). *How to Break a Bad Habit*. Harvard Health Publishing

14. Janson. (2022). *Change bad habits fight fears & anexity with psychology, understand your patterns sabotage & inner child, learn to use mindfulness emotional intelligence & anti-stress reslilience* (Janson, Ed.; 2nd edition). Best of HR Berufebilder.de. Change habits, break patterns: embrace your inner child by Cornelia Schenk

15. Mandela, Nelson. (1994). Long Walk to Freedom: The Autobiography of Nelson.

16. Courtwright, D. (2019). *The age of addiction how bad habits became big business.* The Belknap Press of Harvard University Press.

17. Bad habits in children and their impact on oral health and development of teeth. (2020). *International Journal of Pharmaceutical Research, 12*(sp2). https://doi.org/10.31838/ijpr/2020.SP2.172

18. Wood, D., Esplin, C.R., Hatch, G., Dodini, D., Braithwaite, S.R., & Benjamin M. Ogles. (2022). Predicting readiness to change among pornography consumers, Sexual and Relationship Therapy, DOI: 10.1080/14681994.2022.2126451

https://crimesciencejournal.biomedcentral.com/articles/10.1186/s40163-020-0111-2

ABOUT THE AUTHORS

Reginald Wingfield is an apostolic visionary and co-founder of Wingfield Ministries. He has a passion for teaching and working with at-risk youth. Reginald's life has been one of service. He was in the United States Army where he served 15 years as a Squad Leader. Reggie currently works for the Department of Juvenile Justice as an Intake Supervisor. He has an Associate degree from Central Texas College in Criminal Justice, a Bachelor of Science degree in Criminal Justice, and is pursuing his Master's in theology at Liberty University Theological Seminary. Reggie lives with his wife Shanika and their four children in the Carolina's.

Reginald was raised in Albany, Georgia by way of Bartow, Florida. At a young age, he was compelled to join the military in hopes of being disciplined in life and in his professional career. While in the military many core values such as teamwork, brotherhood and professionalism were taught. This skill set created an opportunity to work in the field of Human Services.

Reginald is also a former US Army Veteran who served 15 years in the military. During this time, he was deployed overseas and completed two tours in Operation Iraq Freedom. Reginald taught Basic Rifle Marksmanship, led as a Squad leader, and oversaw combat missions overseas. He completed various military training such as: Combat Life Saver Course, Driver's Training, and other Leadership Development Courses.

In the secular arena, Reginald has worked at several at-risk youth detention centers and private at-risk youth programs. With his tremendous experience with at-risk youth, he is always favored and quickly promoted. His love to teach is evident, and to list all his accomplishments and certifications would be great.

At the age of 18, he knew that God had called him to preach the Gospel. At 21 years old, he felt the need to search God on a deeper level. It was during this time that Jesus was drawing Reggie closer to Him, and closer to his purpose. But like some young men, Reginald ran from his calling for several years. He loved the Lord. He knew God wasn't pleased with his disobedience and finally committed and dedicated his life to be in the will of the Lord. Shortly after he devoted his life to Christ, he found his wife. Reginald states, "I knew I couldn't come at her incorrect. Shanika loved the Lord, and it was written all over her. I knew we would do ministry together. And I also knew that if I didn't have my life together with the Lord, I would have missed being with her!"

Shanika Wingfield is the co-founder of Wingfield Ministries. Shanika has a long history in ministry growing up in the church. She also worked in Kansas, Texas and Florida serving as assistant pastor and Worship leader, alongside her husband, Reggie for over 15 years. Shanika has a Bachelor's degree in Criminology from Kansas State University, a Master's degree in Human Services with a specialization in marriage and families and a doctorate degree in

Educational Leadership, both from Liberty University. She works in many capacities as a counselor, investigator, and author.

Professionally, she has worked with at-risk youth, worked with Child Protective Services of Texas, and as Consulting Clinician counseling at-risk youth and their families in Florida. She is a Family Engagement Coordinator and Certified Adoption Investigator for the state of South Carolina where she counsels with families whose children are in the Department of Social Services custody, as well as an investigator for potential kinship placements.

In August of 2016, Shanika became a published author with her first book, *30 Days of Biblical Affirmations: To change how you look in the mirror.* She is also the co-author of *Cry Baby Faith* and *The Whole Child: Development, Discipline & Destiny.*

This powerful duo is the epitome of what it means to Co-Labor, Co-Minister, Co-Pastor, Co-counsel, and Co-teach! The way they tackle and release the prophetic word or wisdom of God together has not been seen in this generation. Reggie has the Gift of faith and prophecy, and Shanika is a tremendous Seer and Discerner of spirits. Together they love God's people and are on a mission to train people wholistically. Reggie and Shanika have made it their life-long mission to call-forth, equip, and send out the people of God into their purpose.

They are true teammates. They love being with one another and it is evident when you meet them. They are full of God's joy and love. They are the proud parents of 5 beautiful children, Destiny, Azariah, Jael, Little Reggie II, and Thomas-James "TJ" Wingfield.

And the very proud parents of a four-legged cockapoo named Legend!

For more information or to request training or interview,
Call 980-216-8858, Email at <u>wingfieldministries1@gmail.com</u>
or write Wingfield Ministries at 2217 Matthew Township Parkway
Suite D-267, Matthews, NC 28105.

Made in the USA
Columbia, SC
28 May 2024